DECORATIVE IRONWORK OF THE MIDDLE AGES AND THE RENAISSANCE

Jakob Heinrich von Hefner-Alteneck

DOVER PUBLICATIONS, INC.
Mineola, New York

Copyright

Copyright © 1996 by Dover Publications, Inc.
All rights reserved under Pan American and International Copyright
Conventions.

Published in Canada by General Publishing Company, Ltd., 30 Lesmill Road,
Don Mills, Toronto, Ontario.
Published in the United Kingdom by Constable and Company, Ltd., 3 The
Lanchesters, 162–164 Fulham Palace Road, London W6 9ER.

Bibliographical Note

This Dover edition, first published in 1996, is a republication of the basic 84
plates from *Serrurerie, ou les Ouvrages en Fer Forgé du Moyen-Age et de la
Renaissance* (French edition—published by Librairie Tross, Paris, 1870—of a
German work). The Publisher's Note was written specially for the Dover edition.

Library of Congress Cataloging-in-Publication Data

Hefner-Alteneck, Jakob Heinrich von, 1811–1903.
  [Eisenwerke, oder, Ornamentik der Schmiedekunst des Mittelalters und der
Renaissance. English]
  Decorative ironwork of the Middle Ages and the Renaissance / Jakob
Heinrich von Hefner-Alteneck.
       p.   cm.
  ISBN 0-486-29260-6 (pbk.)
  1. Ironwork, Medieval.   2. Ironwork, Renaissance.   I. Title.
NK8208.H413   1996
739.4′709′02—dc20
                                                                                    96-9347
                                                                                      CIP

Manufactured in the United States of America
Dover Publications, Inc., 31 East 2nd Street, Mineola, N.Y. 11501

PUBLISHER'S NOTE

The art of ironwork flourished in Western Europe during the Middle Ages and Renaissance. Initially it was used primarily for purposes of protection: hinges, latches, grilles and locks, in addition to door pulls and knockers. Gothic art manifested itself in the elaborate foliate motifs to which wrought iron was particularly adaptable in the hands of the craftsman. The most outstanding examples of these works are frequently ecclesiastical.

The plates reproduced in this volume are taken from *Serrurerie, ou les Ouvrages en Fer Forgé du Moyen-Age et de la Renaissance,* as published by Librairie Tross, Paris, in 1870. The text of that edition is here omitted, as are two plates of engraved alphabets. The captions, written specially for this edition, are adapted from the French text, a translation from the original German.

DECORATIVE IRONWORK
OF THE MIDDLE AGES
AND THE RENAISSANCE

4 Par: Fuss.

1471.

Iron grille, side chapel, Church of SS. Ulrich and Afra, Augsburg.

1

6 Par: Z.b U.

1502.

I.H. v H=A. *del.*   HP. *sc.*

Lock and handle, door, the former Convent of Landau, Nuremberg.

4 Par: Zoll.

1460 — 1480.

Iron altar candlestick.

3

B.

A.

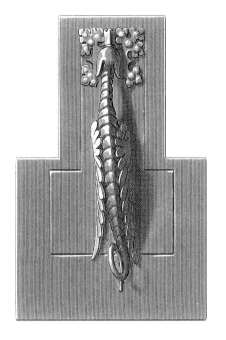

C.

D.

E.

1460 — 1480.

I H v H=A .del .   H. sc .

Padlocks.

1460 – 1480.

LEFT AND RIGHT: Chased and engraved sheet-iron rosettes.
CENTER: Door handle.

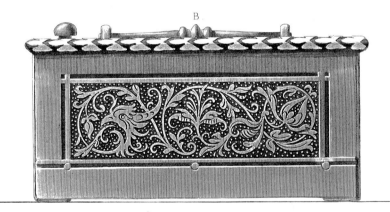

J557

Iron casket with etched decorations.

iP:Z:

Gr.-Gr.

1420—1440.

J.Ha;HEFNER-ALTENECK del.

G.R.

TOP: Rosette door knocker. BOTTOM: Top section of the lock of a chest.

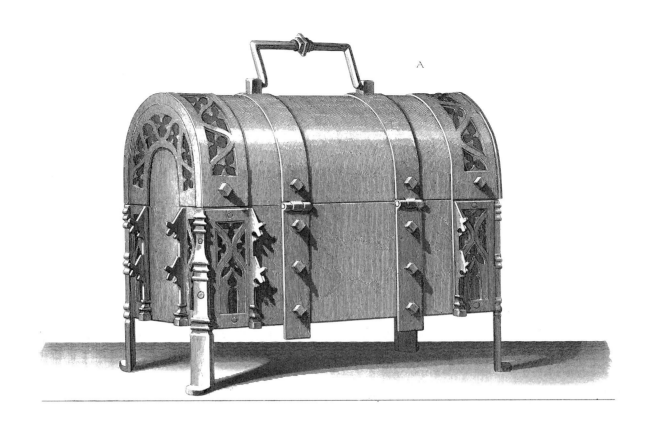

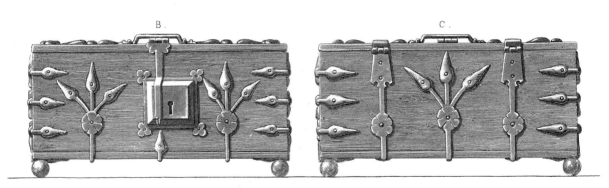

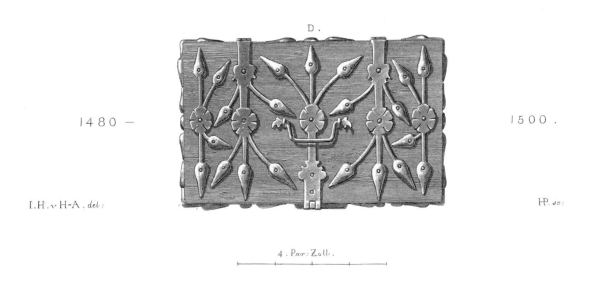

1480 —   1500.

L.H. v H-A . del: H.P. sc:

4 . Par: Zoll .

Money boxes. A: Iron box. B–D: Wooden box with iron fittings.

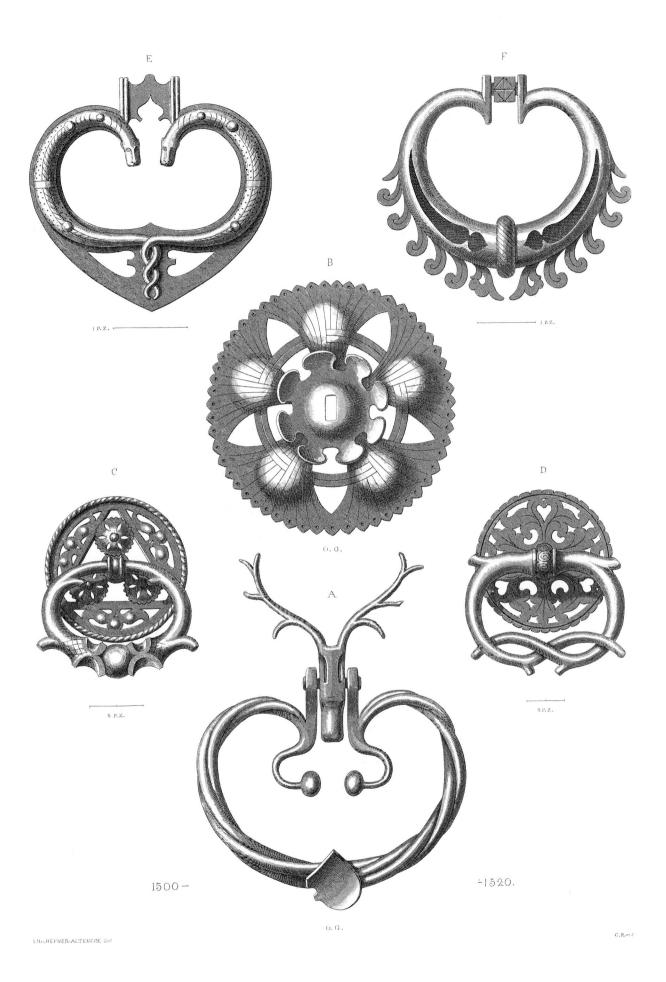

E

F

B

C

D

A

1500—

—1520.

O.G.

2 P.Z.

2 P.Z.

1 P.Z.

1 P.Z.

O.G.

J.H.v.HEFNER-ALTENECK del.

C.R.sc.

Door knockers and handles.

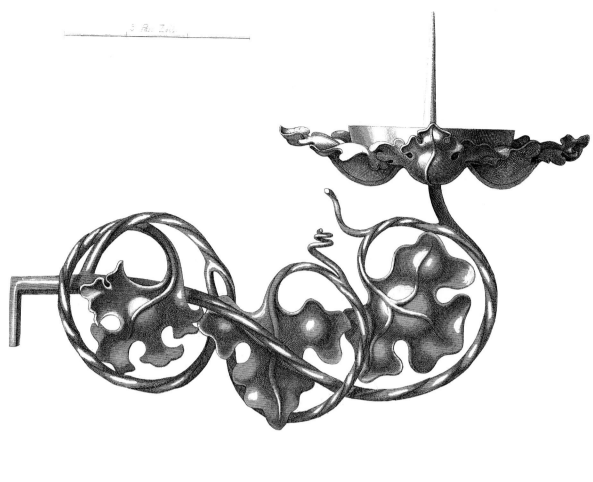

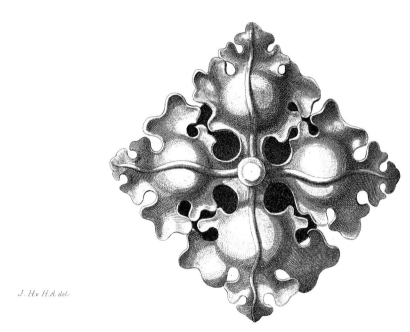

1480 — 1500

Iron candle bracket in the shape of a branch with foliage.

A.

6. PAR. ZOLL.

B.

4 P. Z.

C.

4. P. Z.

D.

GERMANIA

E.

F.

2. Par. Zoll.

I. H. v. Hefner=Alteneck. del.

1600 — 1620.

I. Klipphahn. sc.

TOP: **Hinges.** BOTTOM, LEFT AND RIGHT: **Keys.**
BOTTOM, CENTER: Iron furnishing or door grate.

11

1600 — 1620.

12

Bell frame.

TOP: Hinge of an armoire. BOTTOM: Door hinge, church of Viersen.

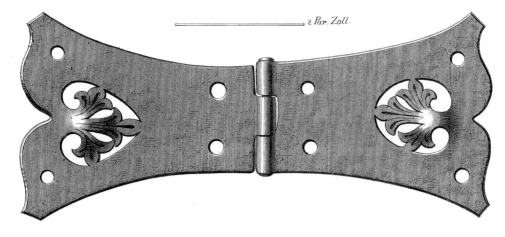

1480 — 1500.

TOP: Hinge with cut and repoussé decorations.
BOTTOM, LEFT AND RIGHT: Keys. BOTTOM, CENTER: Hinge to a chest.

A

B

C

1460 - 1480.

J.H. v. HEFNER=ALTENECK del. C. REGNIER sc.

Ornaments on borders of chest locks.

1440 — 1460.

I.H.v.H=A.del.   I. KLIPPHAHN. sc.

Ornament with openwork repoussé foliage.

A.

C.

E.

3 Par. Zoll

B.

D.

1600 — 1620.

I.H.vH=A.del:

H.P.sc:

Wrought-iron candlesticks.

17

A.

B.

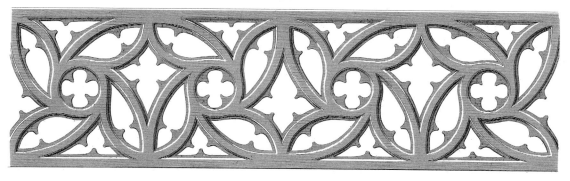

C.

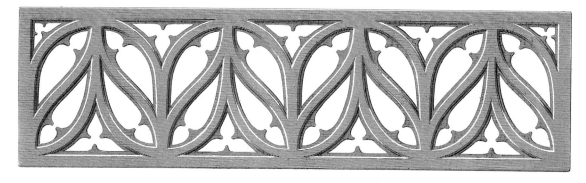

D.

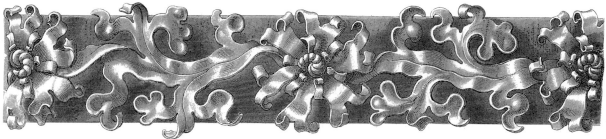

E.

2 Par. Zoll.
ad A

6 Par. Zoll.
ad B

1440 — 1460.

4 Par. Zoll.
ad C

2 Par. Zoll.
ad D

I. H. v H=A. del:

HP. sc:

Iron grilles.

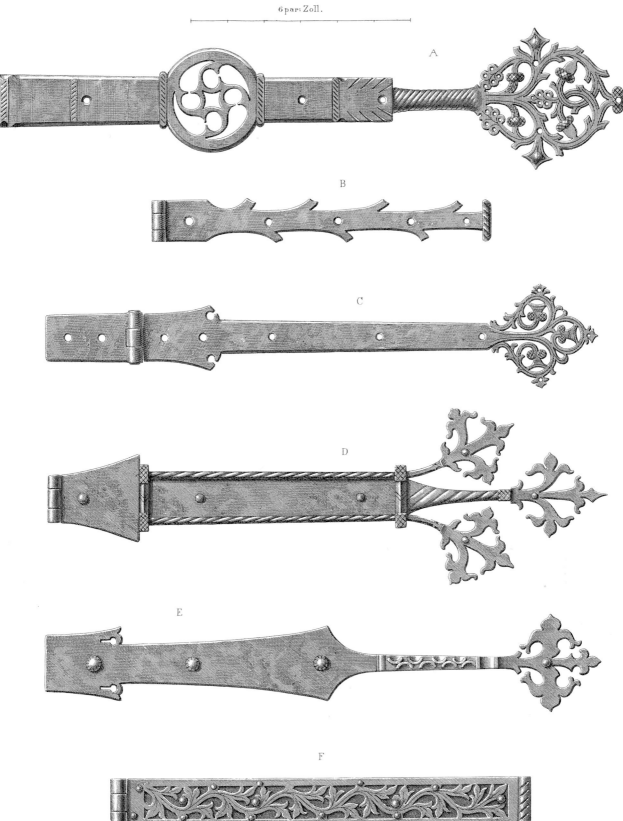

A

B

C

D

E

F

I.H. v. HEFNER-ALTENECK del. 1480 – 1500. C.REGNIER sc.

Door hinges.

E.

D.

F.

6 P.Z.

2 P.Z.

6 P.Z.

G.

A.

H.

6 P.Z.

6 P.Z.

C.

L.

K.

I.

2 P.Z.

2 P.Z.

2 P.Z.

M.

B.

N.

2 P.Z.

1 P.Z.

2 P.F.

1590

IP. del. et sc.

Door knockers, door hinges, locks, etc. from the house (center)
on the Panierberg, Nuremberg, built by the Toppler family in 1590.

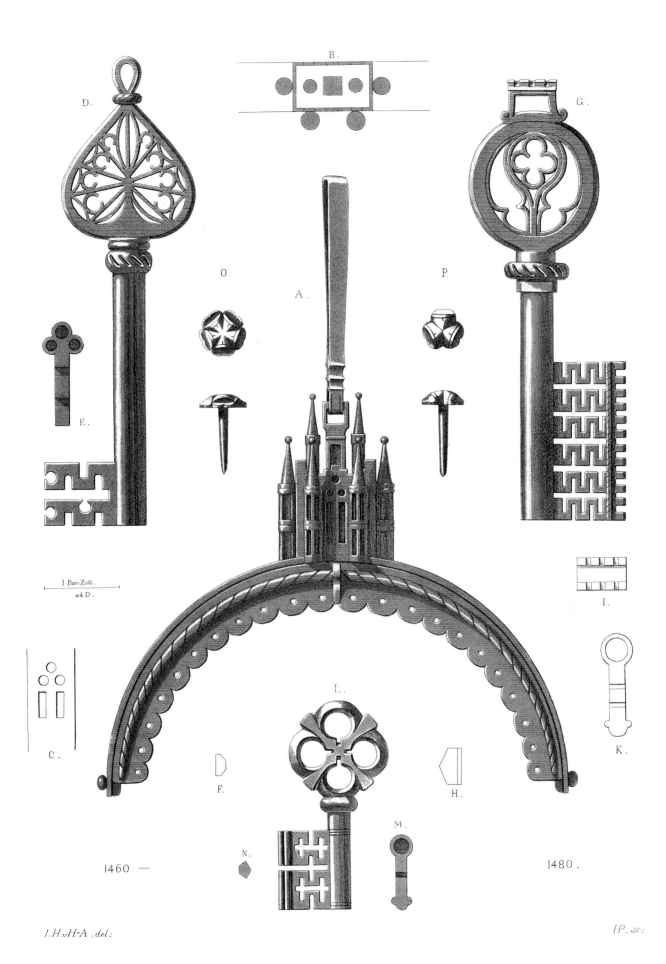

Keys, decorated nails and clasp of a woman's purse.

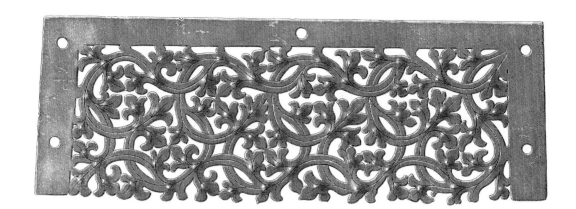

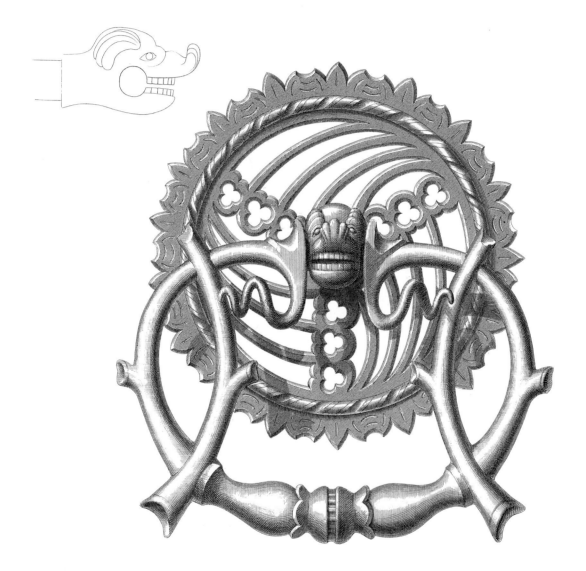

1500 — 1520.

TOP: Top of the lock of a chest. BOTTOM: Door knocker.

A

B

1 4 6 0 — 1 4 8 0 .

I . H . v . Hefner=Alteneck . del .

Ioh . Klipphahn . sc .

TOP: Covering of the lock of a chest, cut out, repoussé
and embellished with lines. BOTTOM: Lock of a chest.

23

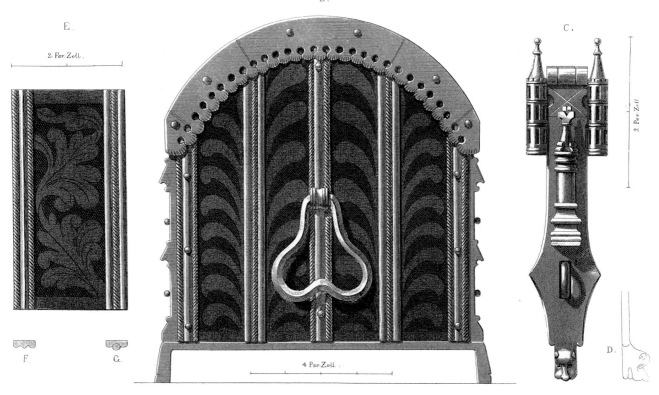

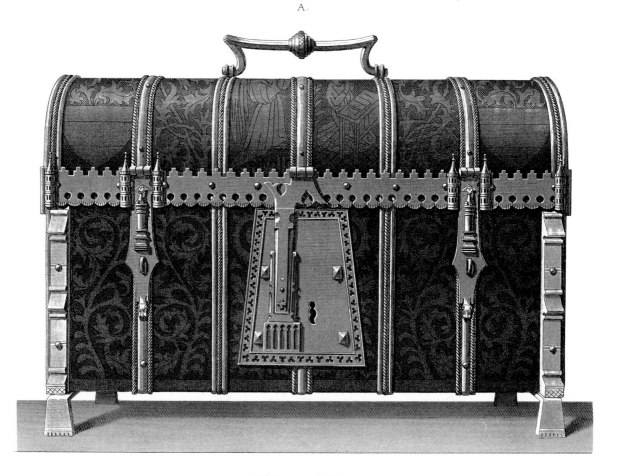

B.

E.

2. Par. Zoll.

C.

F.   G.

4 Par. Zoll.

D.

A.

I. H. v H=A. del.

1380 — 1400

H. sc.

24

Leather-covered wooden casket with iron fittings.

1 P.Z.

A

E

1 P.Z.

F

1 P.Z.

B
1 P.Z.

C

G

1 P.Z.

D
1 P.Z.

H

1 P.Z.

Jos.HEFNER-ALTENECK del.   1500 -   -1520.   C.R. sc.

Ironwork.

25

C .

A .

D .

B .

1 . Par: Zoll .

1 . Par: Zoll .

1500 — 1520

I H . v H A . del :

H . sc :

Ironwork.

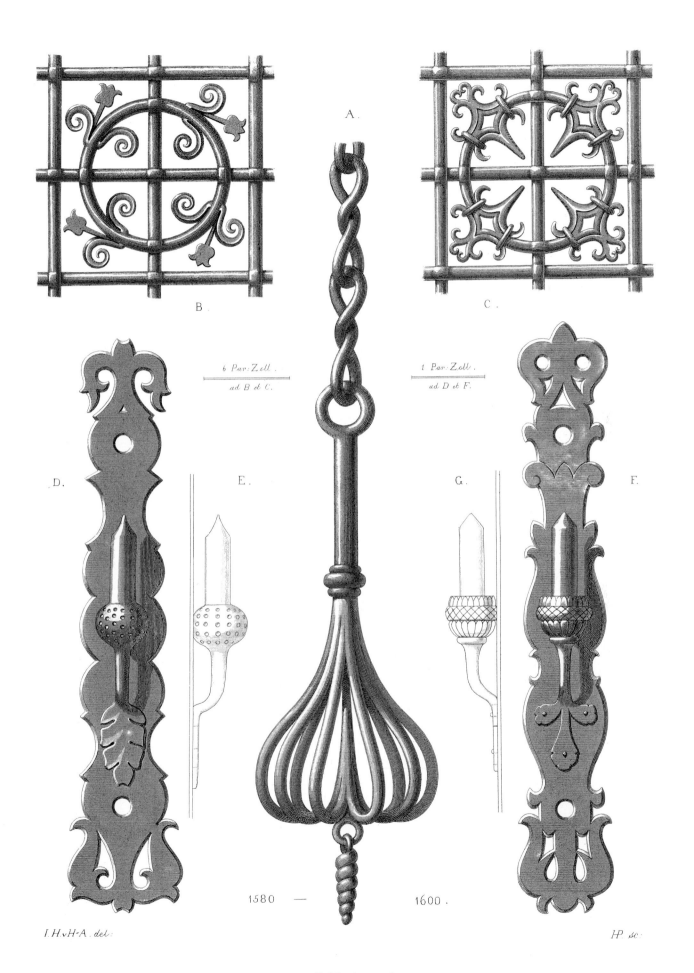

A.

B.

C.

6 Par: Zell.
ad B et C.

1 Par: Zell.
ad D et F.

D.

E.

G.

F.

1580 — 1600.

I. H. v H-A. del.

HP. sc.

TOP, LEFT AND RIGHT: Grille decorations.
BOTTOM, LEFT AND RIGHT: Hinge posts. CENTER: Bell pull.

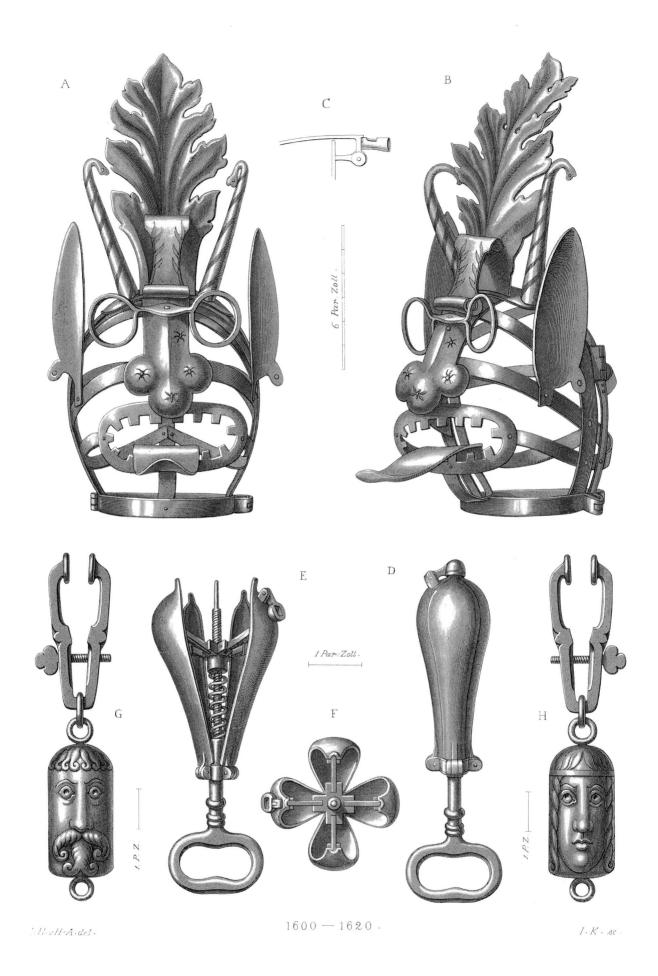

A   C   B

6 Par: Zoll.

E   D

1 Par: Zoll.

G   F   H

1. P. Z.   1. P. Z.

1600 — 1620.

Hollr A. del.   I. K. sc.

Punishment mask and instruments of torture.

A

B

l.H.vH=A.del.

1540 — 1560.

J.K.

Spice mill with engraved decoration.

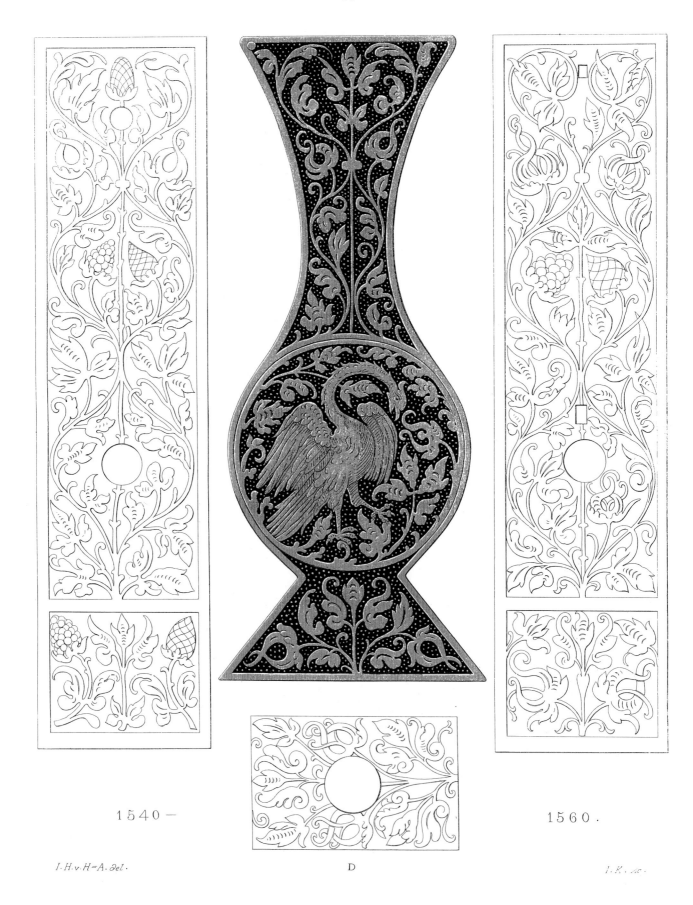

A.

1540 —

D

1560.

I.H.v.H=A.del.

I.K.sc.

Spice mill with engraved decoration (the other side of the preceding).

B

A

D

𝒜ð·A.
1 Par·Zoll.

𝒜ð·B.
1 Par·Z.

𝒜ð·D.
2 Par·Z.

C

J.H.v.H=A. del.

1480 —

1500.

J.K.

TOP: Door pull of an armoire. CENTER: Door hinge of an armoire.
BOTTOM: Door knocker, Bruges.

31

2 PAR: ZOLL.

1460 —   1480

3 PAR: ZOLL.

Armoire door hinge, door pull.

32

1. PAR. FUSS.

1460 — 1480.

Door hinge, Frauenkirche, Oberwesel.

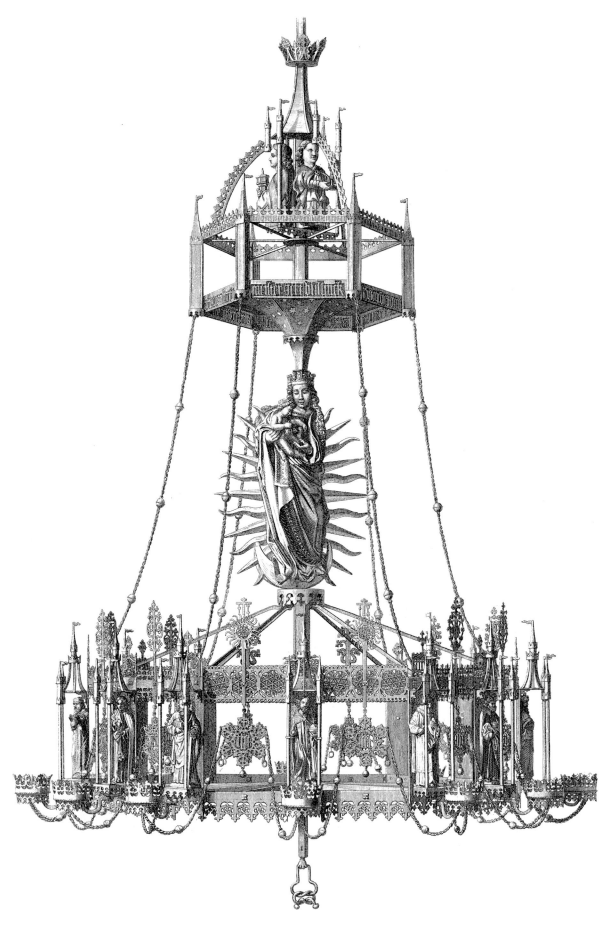

1489.

Wrought-iron chandelier, church of Vreden, Westphalia.

A.   B.

1489.

Details, wrought-iron chandelier, church of Vreden, Westphalia.

35

Details, wrought-iron chandelier, church of Vreden, Westphalia.

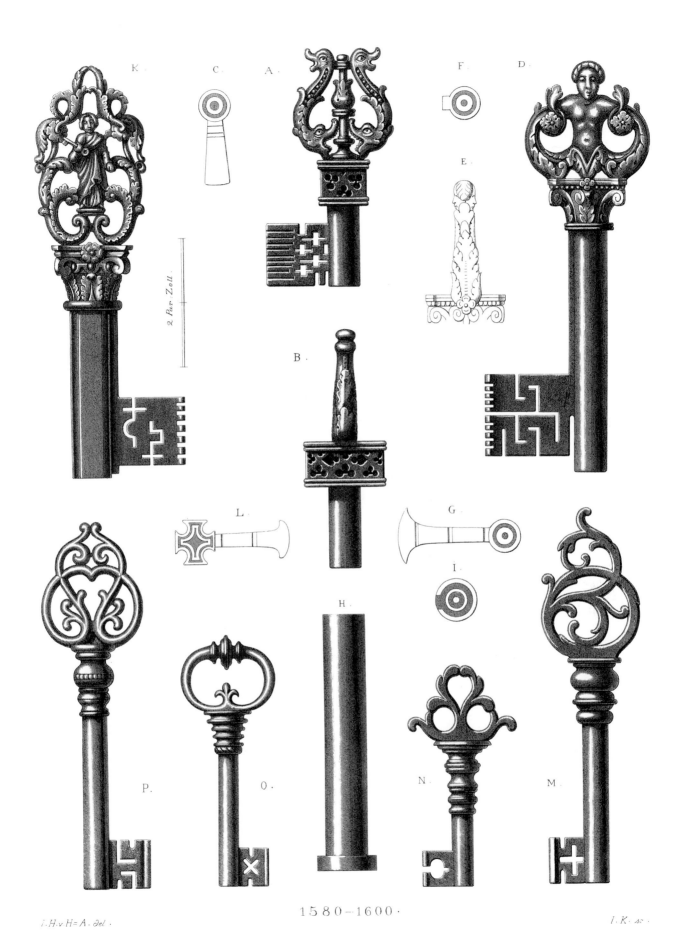

K. C. A. F. D. E. B. L. G. I. H. G. P. O. N. M.

2 Par. Zoll.

1580—1600.

i. H. v H = A. del.

i. K. sc.

Decorated keys.

A.

B.

C.

4 Par. Zoll.

1500-1520.

1 Par. Zoll.

4 Par. Zoll.

I. H. v H=A. del.

I. K. sc.

TOP: Ironwork sign, the mansion called the Stern, Landshut.
BOTTOM: Ornamental rosettes used as the base of door pulls.

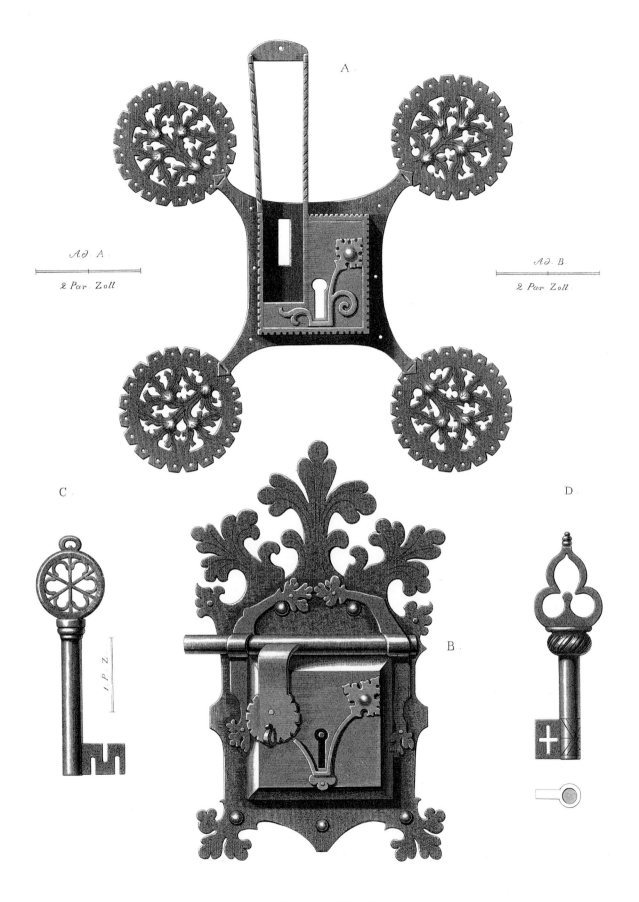

A

C.

D.

B

1480 — 1500.

Locks and keys.

A.

B.

C.

D.

1 H v H A del

2 PZ

3 PZ

4 PZ

1580 —

4 Par Zoll

1600

Iron door fittings.

Ironwork, keyhole plates, keys and door pulls.

1580 — 1600

TOP, LEFT AND RIGHT: Damascened-iron scissor sheath.
TOP, CENTER: Small openwork iron box for perfumes.
BOTTOM: Venetian mirror bordered in damascened iron, front and rear views.

B.   A.   C.

1 Par. Z.   1 P. Z.

D.   E.

2 Par. Z.   1 P. Z.

F.   G.

2 Par. Zoll.

1480 – 1500.

I. H. v H=A. del.   I. K. sc.

1 P. Z.   3 P. Z.

TOP, LEFT AND RIGHT: Bases of door knockers. OTHERS: Door pulls.

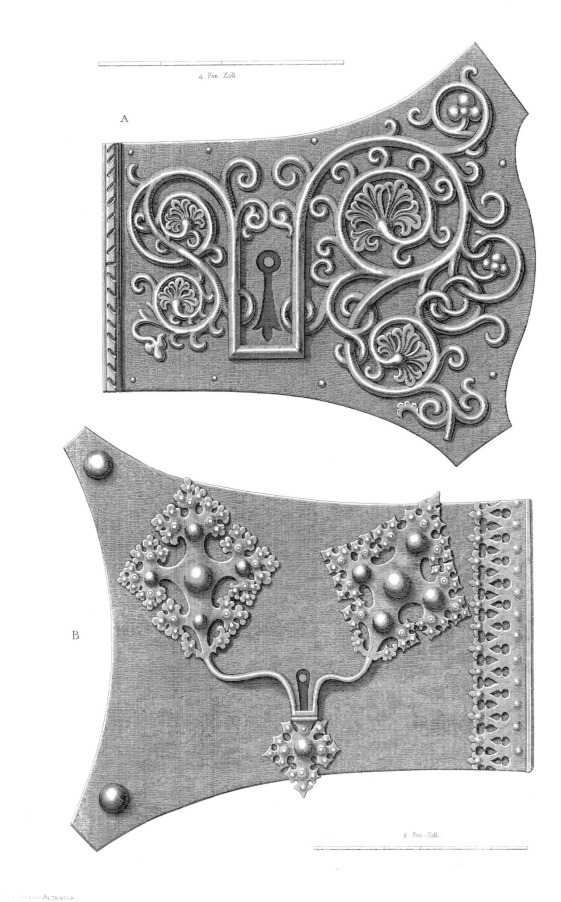

A

B

4 · Par · Zoll ·

6 · Par · Zoll ·

1 4 3 0 — 1 4 4 0 ·

Locks.

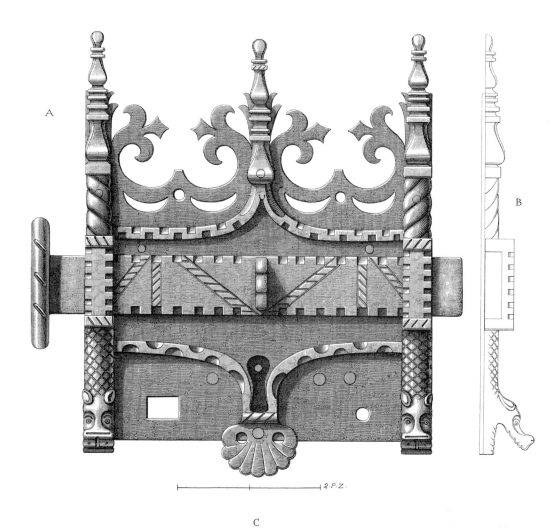

A

B

2·P·Z·

C

J. H. v. Hefner=Alteneck. del.

3 Par. Zoll.

J. Klipphahn. sc.

1460 — 1480.

TOP: Lock with bolt. BOTTOM: Top of a lock.

1460 - 1480.

A

z par: Zoll.

B

Door knocker.

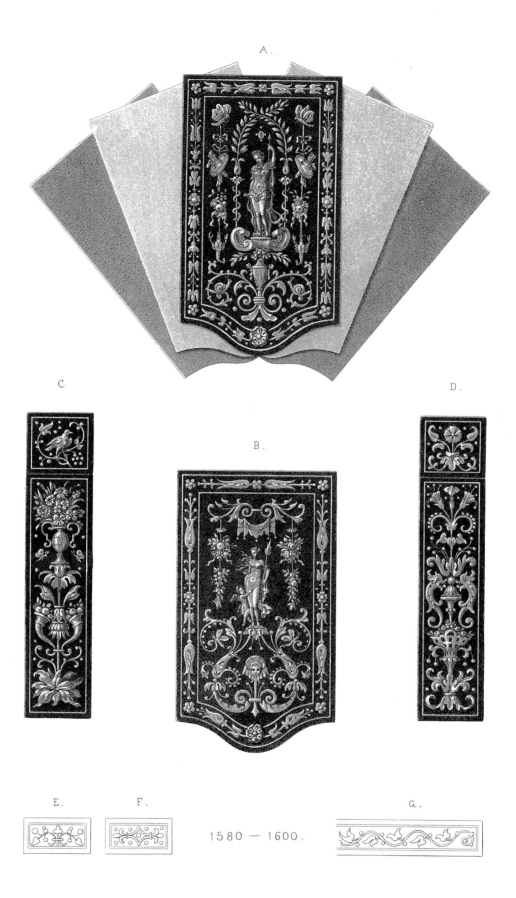

A.

C.   D.

B.

E.   F.   1580 — 1600.   G.

Iron case for pins and memoranda, damascened in gold and silver.

B.

3 P.Z.

A.

C.

2 P.Z.

D.

1 P.Z.

E.

1 P.Z.

F.

2 Par. Fuss.

1380 — 1400.

1 P.Z.

G.

1 P.Z.

I. H. v. H=A. del.

I. K. sc.

48   TOP, LEFT AND RIGHT: Keyhole plates and keys.
TOP, MIDDLE: Iron-clad door.
BOTTOM, LEFT AND RIGHT: Nails used in bookbindings.

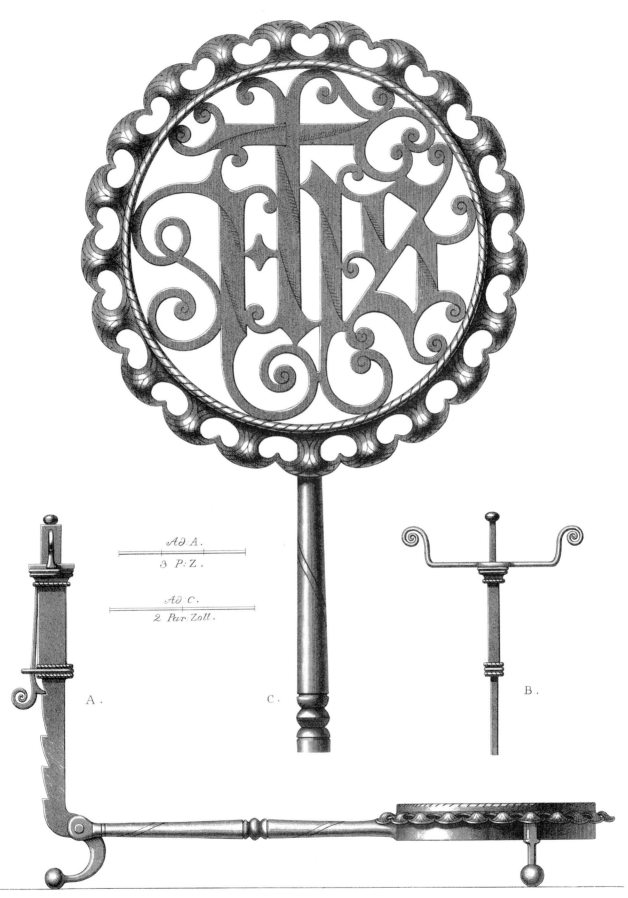

A.

C.

B.

𝒜∂·𝒜.
3 P:Z.

𝒜∂·C.
2 Par·Zoll.

I.H.v.H=A.∂el·   1480 — 1500·   I.K.∡c.

Trivet for a frying pan.

4 Par:Fuss.

1620 — 1640

50

Iron grille from a tomb.

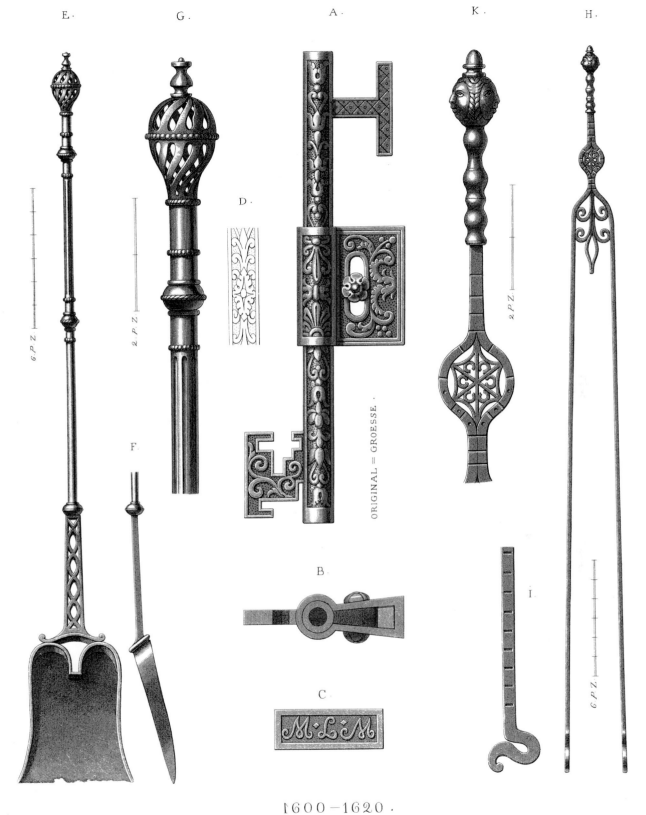

E.   G.   A.   K.   H.

D.

6 P Z

2 P Z

ORIGINAL = GROESSE.

2 P Z

F.

B.

C.

M·L·M

I

6 P Z

1600—1620·

I·H·v·H=A. del·

I·K· sc·

LEFT: Shovel. CENTER: Double key. RIGHT: Tongs.

51

B.

E.

F.

C.

D.

A.

3 P.Z — ad A.

4 P.Z — ad B.

2 P.Z — ad C.

2 P.Z — ad D.

2 P.Z — ad E.

2 P.Z — ad F.

I.H.v H=A. del.

1600 — 1620.

I.K. sc.

TOP: Top of a key rack. BOTTOM, LEFT AND RIGHT: Keyhole plates.
BOTTOM, CENTER: Candlestick.

52

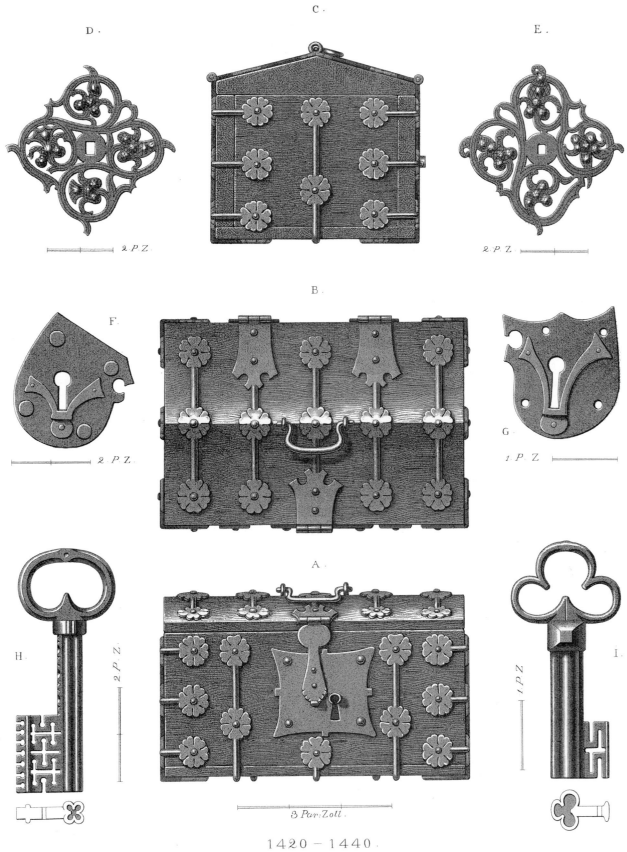

C.

D.

E.

2·P·Z.

2·P·Z.

B.

F.

G.

2·P·Z.

1·P·Z.

A.

H.

I.

2·P·Z.

1·P·Z.

3·Par:Zoll.

1420 – 1440.

I.Hv.H=A. del.

I.K. sc.

LEFT AND RIGHT: Rosettes, keyhole plates and keys. MIDDLE: Iron-clad oak casket.

A.

B.

C.

4 Pariser Fuss.

1160 — 1180.

I. KLIPPHAHN. sc.

Leaf of a door with iron hinges, castle of Brunswick.

C. B. D.

A.

H. E. G. F. I.

K.

i.P.Z.

I. H. v. H–A. del. 1420 — 1440· *I. K. sc.*

TOP: Wooden casket covered in embossed leather, with iron fittings.
BOTTOM: Keys.

55

2 P. Zoll.

B.   A.   C.

H.   I.

E.

D.

F.   G.

I.H. v H=A. del.   1540 — 1560.   I.K. sc.

TOP, LEFT AND RIGHT: Keys. TOP, CENTER: Keyhole scutcheon with the arms
of France and the crest of Diane de Poitiers.
BOTTOM, LEFT AND CENTER: Pull from the door of an armoire.

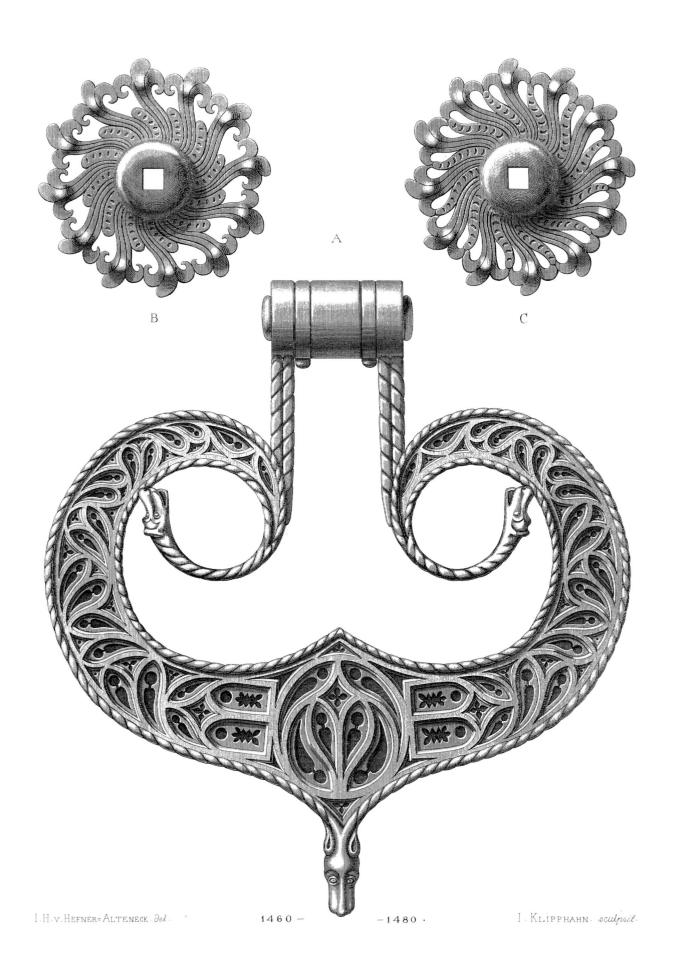

A

B   C

I. H. v. Hefner=Alteneck. del.   1460 —   — 1480.   I. Klipphahn. sculpsit.

Door knocker and ornaments.

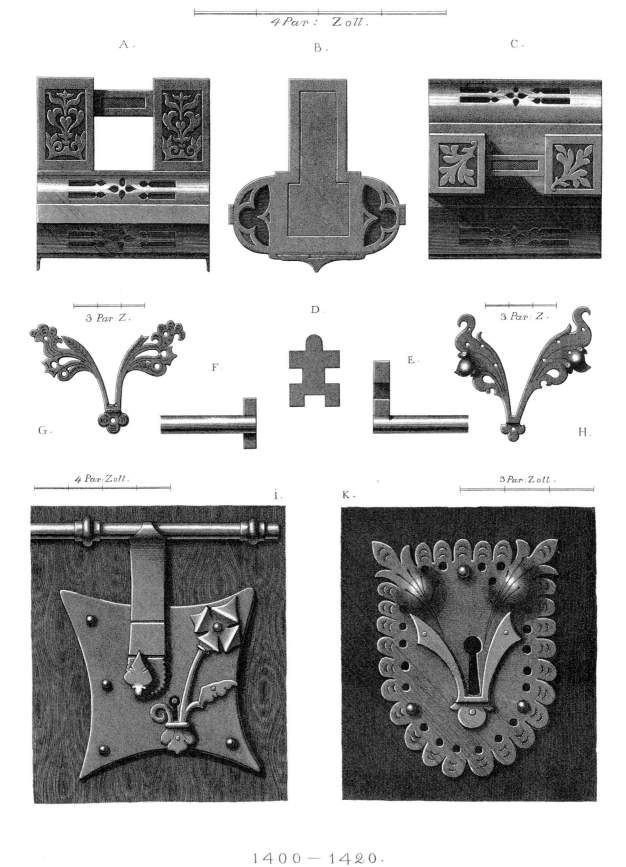

4 Par: Zoll.

A. B. C.

3 Par: Z. D. 3 Par: Z.

F. E.

G. H.

4 Par: Zoll. i. K. 3 Par: Zoll.

1400 — 1420.

I. H. v H-A. del. I. K. sc.

Engraved and ornamented padlocks, keys and ornaments.

F.

G.

D.

C.

A

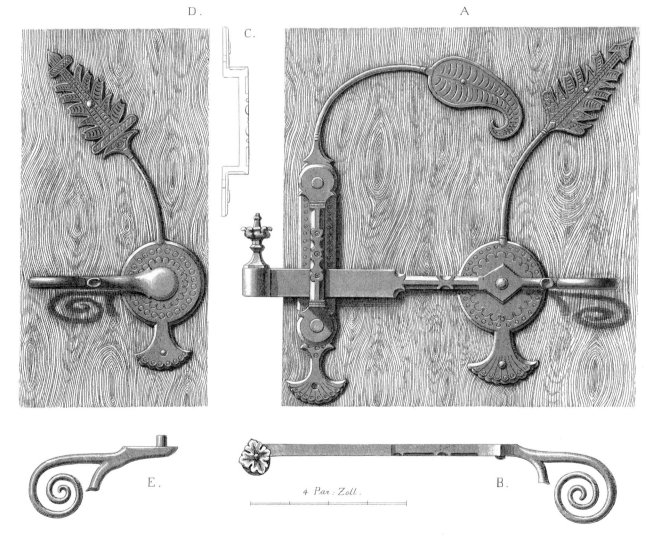

E.

4 Par. Zoll.

B.

J.H. v. H=A. del. 1480 — 1500. H.P. sc.

TOP: Iron decorations from an armoire. BOTTOM: Springless latch.

2 Par. Zoll.

A

B

C

2 Par. Zoll.

J.H.v. HEFNER-ALTENECK del.   1480 – 1500.   C. REGNIER sc.

TOP: Top of a lock. BOTTOM: Door knocker.

I H. v H=A. del.   1180 — 1200.   I. Klipphahn . sc.

Door hinge, Notre-Dame, Paris.

I.H.v.H=A. del.   1180—1200.   I.K. sc.

Door hinge, Notre-Dame, Paris.

LEFT AND RIGHT: Screws and key bows. CENTER: Door knockers.

B.

A.

C.

$A\partial : A$
5 · Par · Zoll ·

! H v H=A . del .   1600 — 1620 ·   I. Klipphahn . sc

Finials.

C

3 p.Zoll.

D

1 p.Fuss.

B

E

1 p.Fuss.

A

3 p.Zoll.

1380 — 1400.

L.H. HEFNER-ALTENECK del.   C. REGNIER sc.

Top of a lock and hinges.

. H . v . H = A . del .   I . KLIPPHAHN . SC .

1 5 0 0 — 1 5 2 0 .

Top of a lock and door knocker.

C.   A.   D.

B.

1 P. Zoll.

2 P. Zoll.

2 P. Zoll.

I. H. v. HEFNER-ALTENECK del.

1580 — 1600.

IOH. KLIPPHAHN sc.

Keyhole plate, door pull or knocker, hinges.

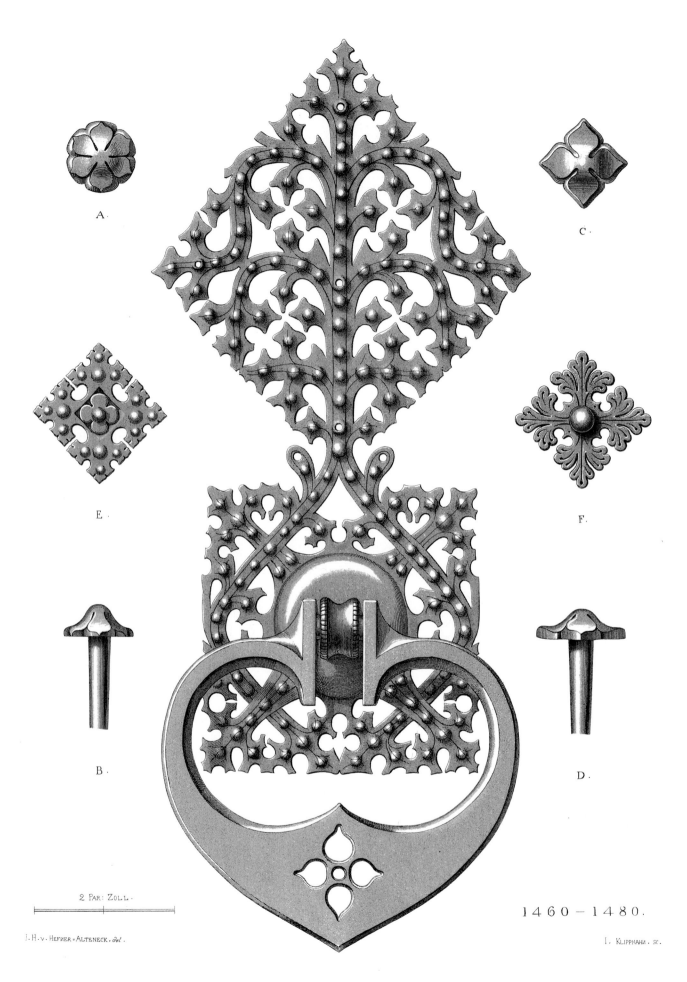

J.H.v.HEFNER=ALTENECK.del.

2 PAR. ZOLL.

1460 — 1480.

I. KLIPPHAHN. SC.

Door knocker and nail heads.

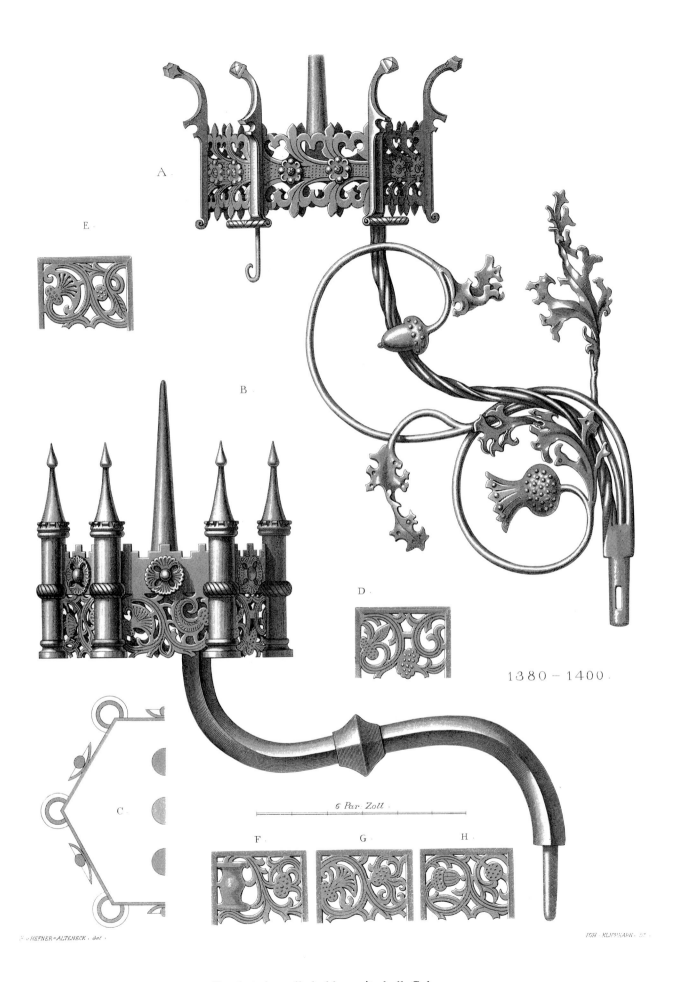

A.

E.

B.

D.

1380 – 1400.

C.

6 Par. Zoll.

F.   G.   H.

. HEFNER=ALTENECK . del .   IOH . KLIPPHAFF . sc .

Bracketed candle holders, city hall, Cologne.

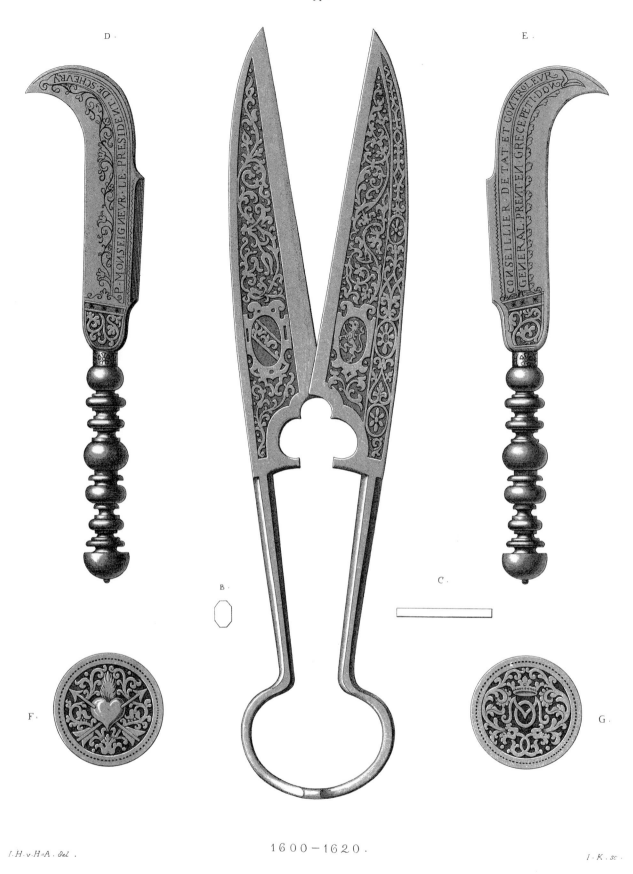

A.

D.

E.

B.

C.

F.

G.

1600-1620.

P. MONSEIGNIEVR. LE PRESIDENT. DE SCHEVRY

CONSELLIER . DE TAT ET COVTROLEVR GENERAL. PREVT. EN. GRECE. PETI. DON

I.H.v.H=A.del.

I.K.sc.

Scissors, pruning knife and small box.

70

4 Par: Fuss.

1640—1660.

J.H.v.HEFNER=ALTENECK. del.
I. KLIPPHAHN. SC.

Wrought-iron grille, cemetery of St. Peter, Salzburg.

2 Par. Zoll

1460 — 1480.

I.H.v.H-A. del.   I.K. sc.

Plate for a door knocker.

72

I. H. v. HEFNER=ALTENECK . del .   IOH . KLIPPHAHN . sc .

Door knocker, second half of the fifteenth century.

A .

B .

3 Par: Fuss.

1600 — 1620

I. H. v. H=A. del.   I . K . sc.

TOP: Iron grille, Notre-Dame, Paris.
BOTTOM: Iron grille, Frauenkirche, Munich.

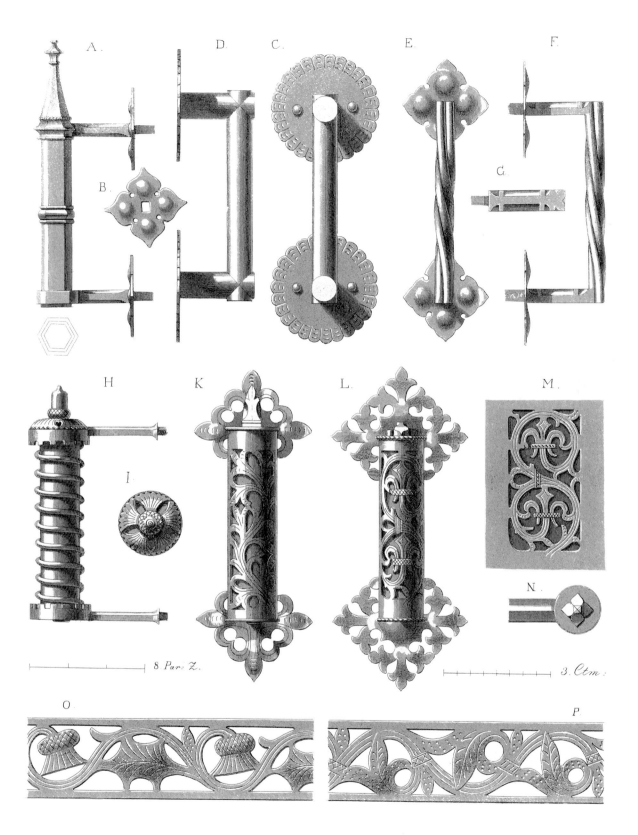

A. B. D. C. E. F. G.

H. I. K. L. M. N.

8 Par: Z. *3. Ctm:*

O. P.

1460 — 1480.

I.H.v.H=A. del: *H.P. sc:*

Door handles and framing borders.

Grave crosses from the cemeteries of the Abbey
of St. Zeno, Bad Reichenhall; Untergeissenberg; Grossgemein.

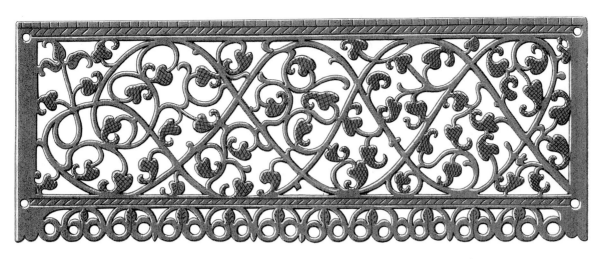

I.H.v H-A. del.   I.K. sc.

1460 — 1480.

TOP: Top of a lock. BOTTOM: Ornament, door panel.

D. A. E.

3.P.Z. 3.P.Z.

B. C.

5.P.Z. 5.P.Z.

6 Par. Zoll.

15 ctm.

I H v H-A. del. I. K. sc.

1640 — 1660.

TOP, LEFT AND RIGHT: **Keyhole plates.** BOTTOM: **Candlesticks.**

A .   2 · P · Z ·   C .   B .

D .

Or · Gr ·

I H v H-A · del ·   1 4 8 0 — 1 5 0 0 .   I · K · sc ·

Door pulls and details of hinges, Archbishop's Palace, Salzburg.

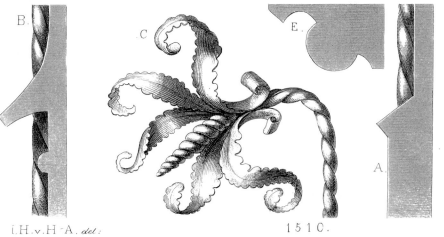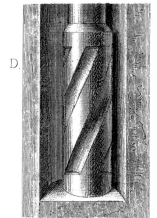

Iron grille with details (fleuron restored), church of Heidingsfeld, near Würzburg.

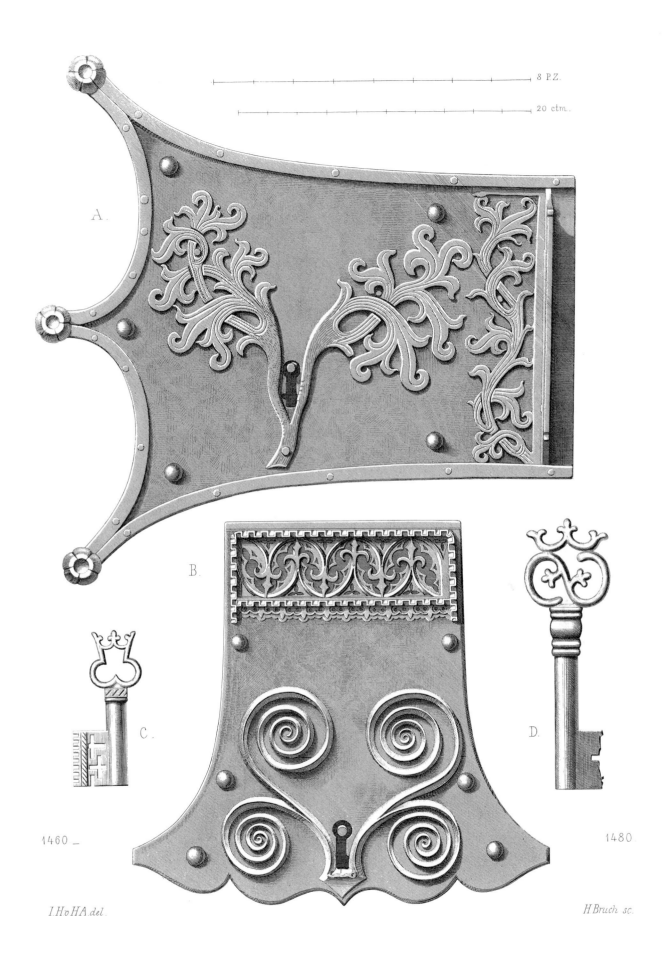

8 P.Z.

20 ctm.

A.

B.

C.

D.

1460 —

1480

I.HoHA.del.

H.Bruch sc.

Keyhole plates and keys.

Details of iron grilles from the Schöner Brunnen, Nuremberg;
keyhole plates and a pull from a small box.

I.H.v.H-A.del.

1600 - 1620.

I.K.sc.

2 Par:Fuss

TOP: Iron grille, former Brandenburger Hof, Amberg.
BOTTOM: Iron grille, Frauenkirche, Munich.

83

A: 1470.

I.H. v.HEFNER=ALTENECK. del:

H.PETERSEN. sc:

Wrought-iron wellhead, Cathedral of the Holy Virgin, Antwerp.